Taurus

2025

(Annual Horoscope 2025)

Dr Gautam DK

Naresh Gautam

First Edition June 2024

Prayer

|| om ga□ ga□apataye nama□ ||

|| brahmā murāristripurāntakārī bhānu□śaśī bhūmisuto budhaśca guruśca śukra□śanirāhuketava□sarve grahā□śānti karā bhavantu ||

Brahmā (the Creator), Murāri (Vishnu, the Sustainer), Tripurāntakarin (Siva, the slayer of the demon Tripurāsura), Bhānu (the Sun), Shashin (the Moon), Bhūmisuta (Mars, the son of the Earth), Budha (Mercury), Guru (Jupiter), Shukra (Venus), Shani (Saturn), Rāhu and Ketu, may all these Grahas be peaceful.

Books by the Author

Table of Contents

INTRODUCTION

As we bid farewell to 2024 and greet the New Year 2025, we embrace the hope that comes with new beginnings. Time is in constant flux, and the future remains a mystery, offering both trials and opportunities. The cycle of time keeps moving, ushering in fresh experiences and transformations.

In the year 2025, hope shines as we continue to recover from the aftermath of the major ups and downs which have impacted businesses, markets, and health worldwide. The ongoing conflicts in Ukraine, Israel – Ghaza etc persisting for long times adds to the complexities of the global situation. Moreover, the pressing concern of global warming is disrupting our natural weather patterns, leading to more frequent cyclones and unexpected floods. Nature's expression through extreme weather events reminds us of the importance of sustainable development and environmental conservation.

Let's explore the significance of the coming year, 2025, based on your Zodiac Sign. Each sign experiences unique outcomes in the upcoming year. What does your Zodiac Sign have in store for you in 2025? What changes will it bring into our lives and what can we expect in areas such as social, political, and others? What lies ahead for you in terms of Education, Love, Marriage, Career, potential career changes, job promotions, business expansion, financial prospects, Health, Property matters, travel to foreign lands, and new ventures?

I would like to cover this annual horoscope in five chapters. In the first chapter, we will cover the transit of planets in the year 2025 and its implications mundane level. How the movement of planets is going to affect the world on various front as world economy, politics, finances, food production, tourism and healthcare. In the second chapter, we will cover the important dates during which major events at mundane level will happen. These two chapters will be common for predictions for all zodiac signs.

In the third chapter, we will cover the basic characteristics of a particular zodiac sign. In the fourth chapter, we will cover the Year 2025 as a whole for that zodiac sign. It will be based on the transit of major planets and conjunctions affecting for a longer duration. In this chapter we will be covering the Year 2025 predictions in terms of general, profession, finances, health, love life and marriage, progeny, education and spiritualism.

In the fifth chapter we will go through month wise predictions for the zodiac sign. These predictions will be primarily based upon transit of Sun and then effect of other planets. This will be precise to plan the activity every month. In the sixth chapter, we will recommend few remedies which will help to mitigate the negative effects of major planets. In the appendix, we will be giving details of transit of planets in the year 2025, various conjunctions formed thereon and eclipses in the year 2025.

From Aries to Pisces, every sign will experience different opportunities and challenges, tailored to their personality traits. Get ready for the ups and downs of life as we reveal what the stars have in store for you.

Astrology is an ancient art and science that has guided humanity for centuries. It provides a deeper understanding of ourselves and the world. Our goal is to empower you with knowledge, helping you make informed decisions and avail the opportunities in 2025.

Events in a person's life are indeed influenced by the positions of planets in their birth chart. The timing of these events is determined by the planetary periods (Dasha and Antar Dasha), and the planetary transits indicate when the results of those events will manifest. **If an event is not promised in the birth chart and is not aligned with the current planetary periods, the transits might not have a significant impact.**

The concept of Desh (place), Kaal (time), and Patar (individual) plays a crucial role in shaping the outcomes of astrological influences. Results can vary based on geographical location, time, and the individual's unique circumstances. In our Zodiac, there are twelve zodiac signs, and each sign represents about 1/12th of the world's population. However, it's impractical to think that the predictions based on these signs will apply perfectly to everyone. They cannot be applied to every person with the same zodiac sign. What might be a fortunate time for a wealthy person could translate differently for someone with fewer resources. Even individuals born at the same time (like twins) can experience different life paths due to the interplay of their choices and actions (karma) alongside astrological influences.

Please understand that destiny is a complex interplay of cosmic influences, personal choices, and life circumstances. It's a dynamic interaction that can guide, but not completely dictate, the course of one's life. While the stars influence us, remember, it's our own choices that shape our destiny. Keep in mind that the future isn't fixed, and our decisions create our reality.

As a disclaimer, I would like to mention that the future is unpredictable and even our Rishis during Ramayana times could not predict the future of Maa Sita or Lord Ram. We can only try to predict events based on planetary movements, which are derived from knowledge from scriptures and experience. No one in the world can give assurance that an event will happen and with what intensity. We, astrologers, try to decipher with the best of our capabilities and intentions so that we can guide mankind to prepare themselves.

These predictions are general and offer some caution, warnings, and indications based on the movements of major planets like Saturn, Jupiter, Rahu, and Ketu. Individual predictions depend on the specific positions of planets at the time of a person's birth. For better clarity, it is recommended to consult an astrologer. You should consider this a general guide to make preparations before making major decisions. While astrology can provide insights and guidance, it's important to remember that there might not be remedies for certain fixed or incurable karmic situations, as these are aspects of life that individuals may need to face. Everyone has to burn his karmas to progress further in your meta physical world.

Let's welcome the transformative energies of 2025 and make it a year of growth, joy, and self-discovery. May this book be your guiding light, leading you to your dreams. We wish you a year filled with cosmic blessings and endless possibilities!

****

2025: ASTROLOGICAL OVERVIEW

Based on the position and movement of planets in the year 2025, we need to decipher that how it is going to affect the world on various front as world economy, politics, finances, food production, tourism and healthcare.

The planetary position as on 01 Jan 2025 at 00.01 hrs will be as under:

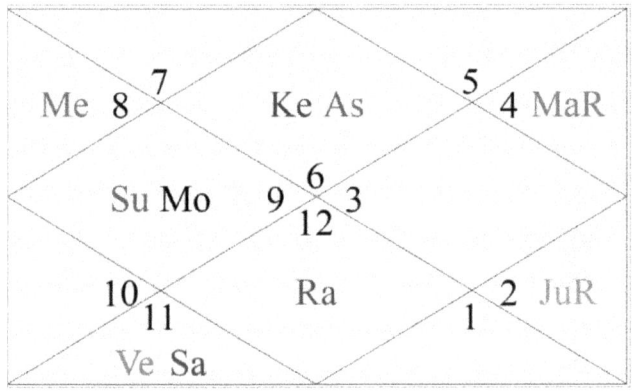

We will go through the transit of planets in the period 01 Jan 2025 to 31 Dec 2025 and try to decipher their implications.

Jupiter in transit in Taurus sign, is retrograde wef 09 Oct 2024 and will be direct on 4 Feb 2025. Jupiter enters Gemini sign on 14 May 2025 and Cancer sign on 18 Oct 2025. Jupiter transit in a sign for about one year and any faster movement, it has to return to that sign. Jupiter become retrograde for a period of 119 days on 11 Nov 2025 and re-enter Gemini sign on 05 Dec 2025. Apart from this, it will remain combust from 22 June to 16 July 2025. During the combustion period, there are no auspicious functions planned.

Saturn is in transit in the Aquarius sign in the year since 2023. It will transit to Pisces sign on 29 Mar 2025. Saturn goes for retrogradation from 13 July 2025 to 28 Nov 2025 for a period of 139 days. With Saturn transit in Aquarius since 2023, Sade Sati is going on for Pisces, Aquarius and Capricorn signs. These three signs are facing a lot of problems and obstacles in their life due to Saturn's Sade Sati effect. Saturn will transit to Pisces on 29 Mar 2025. With this Sade Sati of Capricorn will be over but Sade Sati for Aries will begin.

During this period, Mars will be retrograde in Cancer from 7 Dec 2024 and re-enter in Gemini sign on 21 Jan 2025. Mars become direct on 24 Feb 2025 and transit to Cancer sign on 3 Apr 2025, Leo on 7 June 2025, Virgo on 28 Jul 2025, Scorpio on 27 Oct 2025, Sagittarius on 7 Dec 2025.

Details of Venus and Mercury transit are given at the end of the book.

Venus will be retrograde from 2 Mar to 13 Apr 2025. I find that Venus's signs Libra and Taurus will remain free from any major afflictions of Saturn, Rahu and Ketu in 2025. Something to celebrate for people of these signs. On 25 Mar 2025, Saturn will transit to Pisces and aspect the Taurus sign.

Mercury will be retrograde from 15 Mar to 07 Apr 205 in Pisces, 18 July to 11 Aug 2025 in Cancer,10 Nov to 29 Nov 2025 with transit from Scorpio to Libra on 23 Nov 2025.

Mercury generally retrogrades for the period of 20 to 24 days. During the retrogradation of Mercury, there may be a reversal in actions and speech, indicating shifts in speech abilities, communication skills, and decision-making abilities. People will tend to display either highly introverted or highly extroverted behaviour. They may tend to express themselves excessively or may struggle to express themselves at all. At times, they can make unpredictable decisions or sudden decisions that surprise others. Period 15 Mar 2025 to 07 Apr 2025, when Mercury conjuncts with Rahu and later on 18 Mar 2025, Saturn Joins, the period will be quite challenging as the decisions made during this period may turn to be disastrous.

In the year 2025, there will be two lunar (13-14 Mar 2025, 07-08 Sep 2025) and two solar (29 Mar 2025, 21 Sep 2025) eclipses. Details is given at the end of the book. These eclipses assume importance and can cause various unpleasant events in the world. You may observe incidents within 20-30 days of their occurrence.

Geopolitics

Countries and political parties will make new alliances. You will find major shifts in existing alliances as enemies of one time may become friends. I find India's relations with Western countries further improving after June 2024. Even after 14 May 2025, once Jupiter moves to Gemini, India continue to grow as more responsible and powerful country. Other countries may look to India for guidance and help and India emerge as stronger. India will be treated as Vishwaguru, or a guide or someone who is able to resolve conflicts between the countries. India may initiate talks with Pakistan or will provide some relief during its crisis.

You may notice that during this period, the religious conversion issue will be in focus. Till 18 May 2025, Rahu in Jupiter house is indicative of large-scale conversions to the religious belief system. This may be by force or luring them with money or indoctrination by their religious leaders. fundamentalists will try to hijack the agenda and dominate the government and public. Demand for a separate homeland or to implement laws based on religion will increase causing protests in several countries. Religious fundamentalism will rise further and start disturbing the law and order of many countries.

After 18 May 2025, few countries or religious lobbies may ally to counter the religious fundamentalist forces. There may be a further rise of ISIS or any new organisation or some Christians may rise against Muslim fundamentalism. Few countries may look seriously at the refugee issue and may take some strong action. Governments will try to control the religious conversion momentum.

During the period Mar 2025 to July 2025, one solar and one lunar eclipse are being observed apart from Kaal Sarp Yoga. It creates a war-like situation between different countries. War may or may not happen but weapon industry lobbies will try to create a situation when countries will increase purchases of weapons and material of destruction.

In my annual horoscope 2024, I have already predicted that The situation may aggravate further resulting in the involvement of more countries in this war. The war is going to be between two different religious ideologies which may have devastating effects.

Collateral damage in Ghaza is likely to create a new breeding ground for terrorism and feed for terrorist organisation like Hamas. Muslim population worldwide is going to create a wave of sympathisers and more countries will get entangled in this. Struggle between Muslim and non-Muslim populations may create a major rift. If the issues are not resolved then you will find a greater number of countries will get involved in this creating a situation of world War and the most probable period is when Rahu and Saturn conjunct in Mar to May 2025.

The collateral damages in Ghaza have given a forum to various groups all over the US, UK and EU countries where they are putting pressure on Govt to cut ties with Israel. Initially, govt ignored those protests but now govts are using force to control those protests. Settlement of Palestine refugees is also become a major issue. Iran also fired at Israel and the UN is trying to put pressure on Israel to stop the war. Though Israel will be completing its offensive in Ghaza liberation of Ghaza from Israel will be an issue of discord which will become a reason for instability in the entire region. There is the possibility of more and more countries getting involved in this turmoil. The situation will be critical during the period Mar to May 2025.

European Union will pass through a difficult phase of staying together as there will be a lot of discontentment and disagreement. The war between Ukraine and Russia may become nonrelevant as Ukraine finally agrees not to join NATO.

India's relationship with the US may be under stress as both countries for their national interests and under pressure from the media may have conflict issues.

Politics

Saturn's position in Aquarius, its Mool-trikona Sign, holds great significance, particularly in areas related to career, government, politics, and foreign affairs. However, there may be ups and downs in political issues from July to November 2025, due to Saturn's retrograde motion. Political parties will develop new strategies and try to destabilise existing elected governments worldwide. Misuse of deep fake videos using AI for propaganda will emerge as another battleground.

Finances and Wealth

Stock markets will continue to grow in the year 2025, as Jupiter is progressing towards the Cancer sign, which is a sign of its exaltation. There will be a surge in economic activities. All sectors will boom and give good results. Jupiter gets exalted in the Cancer sign and as it moves towards its exaltation sign, the financial sector booms. Stock markets and Gold will give good results.

Correction in the stock market will be observed after 11 Nov 2025, when Jupiter becomes retrograde. This correction may be for the duration of five to six months. Then markets will again rebound to new levels. This upward trend may continue till Dec 2026. Thereafter I find the markets will be looking for a correction. Prices of Gold and even property may also rise during the same time frame and thereafter look for correction. That correction may not be instant but at a gradual pace.

The year 2025 will provide much relief to everyone. The economic sector will grow, providing more and more employment opportunities of job. However, the Jobs will be skilled or knowledge-based industry rather than semiskilled. Artificial intelligence will continue to replace the human workforce. Those who upgrade themselves will be able to survive otherwise will perish. The world will continue to depend on unskilled labour, but the demand for the same will continue to fall.

The property market will escalate after May 2025, as Saturn will transit in Pisces and this trend will continue for the next 2.5 years. There may be some correction during the retrograde periods of Jupiter and Saturn.

Tourism

Rahu in the Aquarius sign after 18 May 2025, is quite indicative of increased trends in travels to foreign countries. The trend to visit foreign countries will increase. The business of travel agents and tour operators will outgrow. The travel agencies and tour operators will make a lot of money. However, the public will be looking for countries having cheaper cost of living.

Food production

Rahu transit in Pisces till 18 May 2025, the exaltation sign of Venus indicates an increase in means to enjoyment. Life standards of people will improve as more consumer products will penetrate the markets. On 25 Mar 2025, Saturn will transit to Pisces and aspect Taurus, sign of Venus. Taurus is a sign of the entertainment and food industry. Jupiter presence in Taurus from 01 May 2024 to 18 May 2025 indicates that the entertainment and hospitality business will boom. They may adopt new means to reach the masses, especially after the Artificial intelligence and chat GPT. New platforms will emerge to replace the old systems. All the creator needs to upgrade themselves to meet the technology challenges. This advice applies to all people involved in the entertainment industry and hospitality business.

In 2025, there will be bumper production of food grains as Jupiter will expand the reservoirs of food grains. Technology such as the usage of Drones and genetically modified seeds will enhance food production. The commodity market will get a boost.

However, the production of crops after May 2025 will drop. There may be famine or critical food shortage in a few countries. But the world has become one at the commodity level so famine in one place does not mean much scarcity of food, provided you have money.

Healthcare

Healthcare systems may witness a crash during the period Mar to July 2025 as new bacteria or viruses affecting the digestive system may come up. This disease will affect the stomach and digestion-related issues. The reason may lie in polluted water and air. A lot of people in healthcare will be infected due to this disease. One of the reasons for the spread of the same may be contaminated and infected water or air. The healthcare industry will make a fortune out of this disease. The situation will affect a large population in the world.

Disasters

After 29 Mar 2025, Saturn will transit to Pisces, sign of Jupiter. Pisces is the last zodiac sign, indicating detachment, transformation, expenditure and losses. Saturn placement is not good in the Pisces sign. During Saturn transit in the water sign, you may find cases or increase in hurricanes, cyclones, earthquakes, oil spills, pollution of water, nuclear leakages, pollution of water bodies, deficient rainfall etc.

EVENTS DURING THE PERIODS

12 Feb to 14 Apr 2025

Sun conjunct with Saturn in Aquarius sign from 12 Feb to 14 Mar 2025. Sun is in transit over Saturn indicating the state of disagreement between the public and government. There may be a lot of unrest, agitations and law and order problems. Death of any senior renowned politician can happen during this time. The government may try to implement some orders which are not acceptable to a few sections of society. Resulting unrest.

Rahu Sun conjunct in Pisces sign from 14 Mar to 14 Apr 2025. Saturn joins the conjunction on 29 Mar 2025. Rahu can corrupt the government authorities and they can use their powers arbitrarily without any justifications. Sun Rahu or Mars Rahu conjunction indicates fires, accidents or heat waves. In March – April 2025, again some major tragedy will take place which may be related to water and heat. Terrorist activities or riot-like situations cannot be overruled during this period.

Major Alert: 29 Mar to 29 July 2025

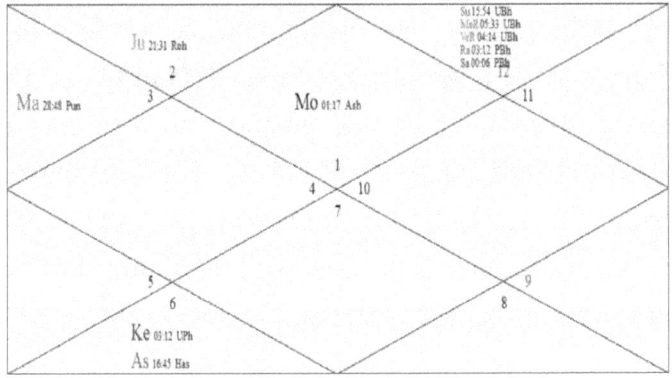

Saturn transit in Pisces on 29 Mar 2025 and conjunct with Rahu till 18 May 2025. This period may be one of the worst, as, during April 2025, Sun, Mercury and Venus will be under the effect of Rahu and Saturn. Mars will be in debilitation and that indicates a major problem at the Mundane level. During this period, there may be major loss of lives, property and human rights due to war between countries, diseases or terrorist action. You may notice that Kaal Sarp Yoga is being formed from 29 Mar 2025 to 29 July 2025. This may be the time when terrorist organisations attack Western countries. Presently, Israel is in the process of finishing the Hamas, a terrorist wing of Palestine. In the process and excessive use of force, there will be a lot of collateral damage. Remember collateral damage creates more enmity and the resultant force emerging is more lethal, evolved and dangerous. Those forces may try to cause a lot of instability worldwide.

If we go down history, the similar planetary position of Kaal Sarp Yoga was formed from June to Sep 2005. Several unpleasant events happened during that period. On 07 July 2005, four coordinated suicide bombings hit central London, killing 52 people and injuring over 700. On 23 July 2005, a series of bombings hit the resort city of Sharm el-Sheikh, Egypt, killing over 80 people. On 14 Aug, a flight crashed in Greece killing 121 passengers and crew. On 16 Aug 2005, another flight crashed in Venezuela, killing 160 passengers and crew. On 29 Aug 2005, Hurricane Katrina made landfall along the U.S. Gulf Coast, causing severe damage, killing over a thousand people and dealing an estimated $100000008 billion in damage. On 31 Aug 2005, a stampede at the Al-Aaimmah bridge in Baghdad, Iraq, killed 953. On 08 Oct 2005, a 7.6 Mw Kashmir earthquake struck Pak Occupied Kashmir, killing more than 86,000 people and displacing several million more.

This time the planet position will be worse when Rahu and Saturn conjunct in Pisces sign and Kaal Sarp Yoga is formed. At the mundane level, there may be several calamities, accidents and disasters. However, life continues as nature destroys to keep a balance in the ecosystem.

15 May to 16 Jul 2025

Jupiter Sun conjunction in Gemini, 15 June to 16 July 2025 will bring positive results for financial sectors. This will be time for the Banking sector to grow and accordingly, stock prices of Banks may notice a spike. This is a time of positivity for the Public. There will be an increase in financial status. Industries will grow with the support of the government. Remember that before this period, there will be a major correction in the market.

07 June to 28 July 2025

Mars Ketu conjunction from 07 June to 28 July 2025 is being formed in Leo sign, fiery sign. Ketu and Mars energies may result in fire, terrorist attacks, and natural disasters in mountainous terrain in a few countries. Leo is a fire sign and Mars is a fiery planet with Ketu, a planet of destruction that will affect nature, forests and land. There may be landslides, and settlement of ground resulting in damage to buildings. Sun and Mars both represent energy. This period also coincides with the summer season when you find fire incidents in several places. This period may also witness air accidents, train accidents, industrial accidents, or major fire incidents.

17 Aug to 15 Sep 2025

Sun and Ketu conjunction is being formed in the Leo sign from 17 Aug to 16 Sep 2025 may bring turbulence for ruling governments. In some states, there may be trading of elected candidates to form various alliances, destabilise the ruling party and form their government. All over the world, you may notice that opposition parties may try to destabilise the ruling government by ethical or unethical means. Terrorist activities will emerge in a new form and higher intensity. Sun is eclipsed by Ketu and indicates trouble in law and order, the death of a popular world leader and an increase in terrorist activities. To control the law-and-order situation, governments have to take some strong steps which can cause mass unrest.

Leo is related to the stomach and digestive system. Diseases related to the stomach may surface as epidemics during this period.

16 Nov 2025 to 14 Jan 2026

Sun-Mars conjunction is being formed in Scorpio and later Sagittarius sign. Sun and Mars energies indicate that the authorities become tyrants and make decisions that may not be democratic or for the welfare of the public. They force their ways to achieve their targets. This period may witness some major clashes between govt and various rebel groups. This may turn out to be violent in Nov 2025. It can have some connection with new laws which will be passed by governments in various countries. Those laws may be against religious conversion or migration-related. Like Europe or Western countries such as the US, the UK may impose certain restrictions on the migration of refugees, population control etc which may give rise to anti-government campaigns. In India, these could be related to the construction of the temple at the site which has been converted to a mosque after the demolition of the temple. Kashi

Vishwanath or Mathura temple may come into focus during this period. Govt may take action on certain parties based on their involvement in corruption or anti-national activities.

I have endeavored to provide predictions for each zodiac sign, which should be considered with both your Moon Sign and Lagna. You can explore how this upcoming transit might introduce new opportunities or challenges in your life and the lives of your family members.

TAURUS SIGN AS A WHOLE

Taurus is the second sign in the series of constellations of the zodiac, located in the Northern celestial hemisphere between Aries to the west and Gemini to the east. It lies between 30 degrees to 60 degrees of Zodiac. In the constellation, Taurus covers three pada of Krittika, complete Rohini and two padas Mrigashira Nakshatras. As per the Sun astrology, people born during the period 20 Apr to 20 May fall under the Taurus sign. Moon exalts in the Taurus sign at exactly 3 degrees. Taurus is one of the three earth signs, alongside Capricorn and Virgo.

Taurus sign ruled by Venus is a female sign, fixed, earth element, cool natured, lord of the direction of south, air character, powerful during the night, auspicious, vaishya caste, and fatigued body. In body parts, it covers the mouth, cheeks and vocal cords.

Alphabets associated with the Taurus sign are A, E, O, Oo, Va, Vee, Ve, Vo, or Wu.

Due to its association with Venus, people born under Taurus are inclined towards enjoying the finer things in life and often channel their efforts into acquiring material possessions and wealth. They enthusiastically pursue anything that brings pleasure, comfort, or financial gain. They have a taste of art, music, food, and luxuries and have an appreciation for aesthetics. Please remember, he may not be associated with all but one of them is a must.

Each zodiac sign is associated with a character or symbol that describes them. The symbol for Taurus is the Bull. Bulls are known for their reliability, loyalty, and determination. The bull is a symbol of strength, tenacity, virility, and power. Taurus personality is thought to be calm and peaceful, but when their anger is aroused, their temper can be wicked.

Being a fixed sign, Taurus natives are practical, grounded, loyal, steadfast, and stubborn. They tend to resist change and they have excellent follow-through. They are happy wherever they are and get agitated when they are required to make some changes. Some key characteristics of Taurus include materialism, greed, patience, practicality, steadiness, and endurance. While they may be somewhat slow, they are committed to completing tasks. Arian may leave a task incomplete but a Taurus individual will be committed to completing the task. They enjoy outdoor activities, physical challenges, and the arts. In love, they are devoted and romantic, emphasizing stable and harmonious relationships.

Being an Earth sign, Taurus are reliable, practical, responsible, patient, stable and sensual. They are known for their perseverance, strength, and sometimes "bull-headed" nature. Taurus individuals exhibit a determined and dogged approach when pursuing their goals. They are characterized by their strong-willed and steadfast demeanour. In addition to their determination, Taurus individuals are known for their sensual nature, enjoying life's pleasures and often indulging in a variety of experiences. Their connection to the Earth element reflects their grounded and practical approach to life.

Taurus individuals methodically have a deliberate mindset, contrary to the aggression associated with their bull symbol. Their sensual nature manifests in a deep appreciation for pleasures such as fine food, luxury, and sexual experiences. They exhibit conservative values, resisting change to maintain a familiar and secure environment. Despite their practical mindset, they may display stubbornness, clinging to established opinions and routines. They are dependable, complete tasks they initiate and value family bonds. As leaders, they seek high esteem and may find collaboration challenging if their leadership is not acknowledged. While their resistance to change can be a drawback, their reliability and commitment make them valuable contributors to various aspects of life.

Taurus sign falls in the second house of the natural horoscope and so, it focuses on understanding the physical world through the senses like taste, touch, sight, hearing, and smell. People with a strong Taurus influence in their birth charts are sensual, deeply connected to physical pleasures, and have a strong attachment to material possessions. Their main principle revolves around the desire to experience things sensually, and they value possession and ownership.

They may take their time to act, but when they do, their actions are thorough and have a lasting impact. They are reliable, prefer familiar company, and can be possessive in relationships due to their need for security. Taurus individuals are patient, contemplative, and calm, but their stubbornness and inflexibility can hinder their progress. They tend to be conservative, and protective and are more inclined towards the familiar than the unknown. Taurus individuals exhibit calmness and perseverance during tough times. However, if they suppress their frustrations for too long, they may explode with intense emotions.

Taurus individuals are characterized by a love for rewards, material pleasures, comfort and the accumulation of various possessions. They are fiercely loyal to their friends but can be burdened by their friends' problems. Taurus individuals tend to be somewhat unaware of themselves and their motives, relying on careful planning and hard work to achieve their goals.

Taurus is often described as the accumulator and builder of the zodiac, with qualities associated with being fixed and earthy. Taurus' love for material possessions and sensual experiences contributes to their desire for the good life. The key phrase for Taurus is "I HAVE!" or "Possessions". Taurus influences a house or planet in astrology charts, as it brings characteristics such as profit, slow but steady progress, determination, resistance to change, dynamism when motivated, and possessive attitudes.

To summarise the positive qualities of Taurus native, he is known for his ability to concentrate and for his tenacity. He is helpful, easily gets along with others, dependable, loyal, and helpful to others. He never leaves anything unfinished but works on something until it has been completed. He is honest, forthright in most of his dealings, practical, thorough and does not believe in shortcuts of any kind. He is deliberate, learns from his experiences, is reliable, tolerant, enjoys peace and harmony with all, becomes part of the team, is supportive of others, is not overly critical and likes people to be themselves. He avoids taking unnecessary risks. He is steadfast. Once his mind is made up it seldom changes. The person born under this sign usually is a good family person-reliable and loving.

To summarise the negative qualities, sometimes the Taurus individual is too stubborn, not ready to accept others' viewpoints, does not like to listen to others, if he has decided, and does not like to be controlled or guided or contradicted. Some people who are born under this sign are very suspicious of others of those persons close to them. They find it difficult to trust people fully. They are not in the habit of forgetting or forgiving. His love of material things sometimes makes him rather avaricious and petty. He does not like changes in his surroundings and gets annoyed if someone disturbs his life.

TAURUS PREDICTIONS: 2025

Taurus is the second zodiac sign, associated with the earth element. People born under this sign are usually practical, determined, reliable and sensual due to their ruling planet Venus. At the beginning of the year, Jupiter in Lagna, Rahu in the eleventh house and Mars in the third house give you a boost in courage and valour, vast social networking and unexpected gains. This will motivate you to pursue various endeavours with great enthusiasm and determination. Saturn in the tenth house indicate gains from profession but after working hard.

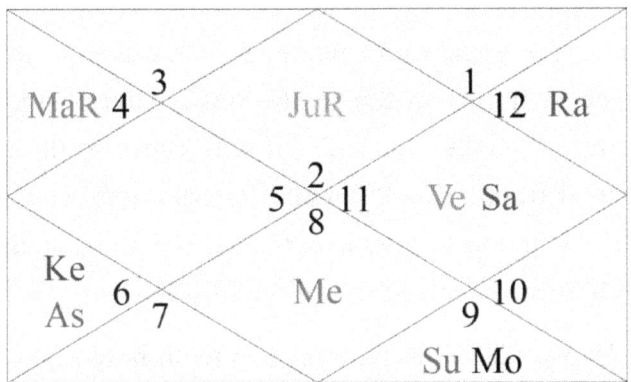

On 14 May 2025, Jupiter will transit to Gemini sign, the second house of chart, which is house of finances. With Jupiter in the second house, the person's finances and career will improve. If you're a business owner, this period might offer opportunities for profit and business expansion. There may be increase in members of your extended family either due to marriage or birth of a child. You will be spending a lot of money for auspicious family function or meeting your responsibility as responsible family member. This Jupiter influence in the second house could also contribute to your success in both work and relationships.

On 18 Oct 2025, Jupiter transit to Cancer, which may be beneficial for any future endeavours and plans. Cancer is the exaltation sign of Jupiter but still you may experience an increase in expenses, pressure in professional areas. You may be required to travel for professional reasons or religious tourism. Jupiter aspect on the seventh, ninth and eleventh house opens the opportunities for Taurus for marriage, gains from life partner and boost the image in Public.

In the first part of year, Rahu in Aquarius in the eleventh house and Ketu in Leo in fifth house bring unexpected gains and vast social network. With the influence of Jupiter on ninth house, Taurus people will find themselves drawn towards a more spiritual path, leading to positive outcomes. Their social network also may be based on higher thinking, spirituality, religion, education or tourism.

Saturn is the yoga karak planet for Taurus sign and till 29 Mar 2025, it will be in transit in the tenth house. This position is good for professional life. After 29 Mar 2025, it will transit to the eleventh house and conjunct with Rahu. This Rahu and Saturn combination from 29 Mar to 14 May 2025 is going to give exceptional results in social networking, gains and this time all your desires will be fulfilled.

After 18 May 2025, Rahu transit to tenth house and is aspected by Jupiter. The period is going to bring great, positive news when it comes to your finances and career. You are going to be blessed with good fortune, and there is going to be a substantial improvement in your financial position. Your relationship with friends and associates will improve invariably. There might be some challenges that you have to encounter in your career, however, there is nothing to be worried about. These hurdles will remain for a temporary period. You have to keep control of your negative thoughts. The year will help you to fulfill your biggest dreams, and you are going to accomplish your greatest achievements. You are advised to have control over your temper, or you might end up losing some favorable connections with your friends and family. You are going to experience a rich period of personal growth and a flourishing career.

Once Saturn goes retrograde from 13 Jul to 28 Nov 2025 and Jupiter retrograde from 11 Nov 2025 to 11 Mar 2026, you will find that problems at financial level and social network level. Rahu being in the tenth house, issues at the place of profession may get activated.

The period 18 Oct 2025 onwards will be conducive to spiritual activities, and you may consider planning visits to religious places. However, be mindful of increased travel expenses during this time.

The period before 14 May 2025 and later after 18 Oct 2025, your bond with your partner will be strong, and both of you will demonstrate loyalty and faithfulness towards each other. This period will bring you closer together, fostering a deeper connection. Any feelings of loneliness you may have experienced in the past will dissipate, and you might find a desirable love partner entering your life. Overall, the year seems promising for personal growth, love, and the fulfillment of long-awaited desires. There are going to be some challenges in your relationship and career. If you lose control of emotions and temper will end up losing everything have been trying to build. Be patient and try to be optimistic.

Profession

Your career and business are off to a positive node, thanks to Jupiter's transit in the Lagna of your chart since April 2024.

Till 29 Mar 2025, Saturn, the Karam Phal Data, will be positioned in the tenth house of your astrological chart. After 29 Mar 2025, Saturn transit to the eleventh house, which is associated with gains, and when Saturn is in its own sign, conjunct with Rahu. It becomes beneficial and will give you success in your professional life. You'll have the opportunity to meet influential people who will impact your career significantly. These influential people may be from different caste colour or community. You may encounter helpful individuals, possibly of the opposite sex, in your workplace who will aid in your professional growth. Learning from these authorities will enhance your efficiency and showcase your talents. Those involved in politics may experience benefits during this period. If you are in politics or social service, then this period can provide you with higher power and authority. Their Social status may find an uplift and those who are in the public domain, in politics, social groups, or on digital media may find a boost in their followers.

Your career and business will get boost as after 14 May 2025, Jupiter moves to the second house and aspect the tenth house. Rahu moves to tenth house on 18 May 2025. Rahu will give positive results in the tenth house despite causing some fluctuations, up and down and uncertainty, because that is the nature of Rahu. Rahu in the tenth house, indicates that you can have growth in professional life by unconventional approach. Rahu is the technology and you have to adopt new technology, make connections with foreign traders, and look for opportunities in the import and export business. There are potential opportunities for financial gain in the business you have been working on, indicating a favorable time to make progress in your professional endeavours.

For those who are doing business in import and export, Rahu connects you to foreign lands and gives a boost to business. You will have the ability to overcome your enemies, although they may continue to pose challenges. Taurus individuals are practical and naturally determined due to Bull type attitude. If they have decided to do something, they will continue to follow that. Due to Rahu aspect on the fourth house, generally native will not get success at his hometown and will be required to travel for his profession.

After 18 Oct 2025, as Jupiter moves to the third house in Cancer sign, you can expect changes in your career. Saturn's transit in the eleventh house, which is the natural house of Saturn and house of gains indicates that your hard work will lead to success only after lot of resistance and continuous efforts. The eleventh house is associated with gains, and when Saturn is in its own sign, it becomes beneficial and will give you success in your professional life. But remember Saturn demand discipline and hard work. You'll have the opportunity to meet influential people who will impact your career significantly.

The period after 18 Oct 2025, holds promising prospects for launching your brand in a different company. Your new business idea is set to progress, and launching your venture will prove fruitful, leading to significant profits. Embrace this success to seek even better opportunities. Nevertheless, there will be challenging days, but don't lose heart; keep moving forward. it could be an opportune time for those considering a career change to act.

Saturn goes for retrogradation from 13 July to 28 Nov 2025 for a period of 139 days. You might face certain hurdles, and gains achieved earlier could be reversed. Beware of potential conspiracies from colleagues during this time, as their support may wane. Be prepared for that and keep your reserves to cater to a rainy day. Jupiter become retrograde for a period of 119 days on 11 Nov 2025 and re-enter Gemini sign on 05 Dec 2025.

During the retrograde motion of planets, results become uncertain and unpredictable. You are advised not to take any hasty decision during that period. Any emotional decision-making during this period may have consequences so make professional choices with care and prudence. Any deal in matters of property, investment, marriage, or family functions needs to be taken without being emotional.

Finances

Jupiter will be in Lagna till 14 May 2025 and then it will transit in the second house till 18 Oct 2025. Thereafter it will transit in the third house.

There will be financial gains from unexpected and unexplained sources during the period 14 May to 18 Oct 2025. Native may gain from secret financial dealings, inheritance, undesirable channels, stock markets, gambling or mutual funds. He will earn from the financial management of other people. This period will be good for long-term investing in the share market as well however retro movement of planets should be considered before making any decision. You may get some ancestral property or gains from stocks, insurance or long-term mutual funds.

I do not find any major undue expenses occurring for Taurus sign as the twelfth house is without any major affliction. The routine expenses can be for family functions, tourism, foreign visits, house renovation or expansion. You may be required to spend some money on your siblings or helping others. There is no need to worry till 18 Oct 2025, as Jupiter will be free from any affliction.

Jupiter become retrograde for a period of 119 days on 11 Nov 2025 and re-enter Gemini sign on 05 Dec 2025. This may be the period which you have to be cautious of any potential losses. During this period, you need to be careful while making any financial decisions However it is advised to not do any panic buying. Any wrong decision taken during this period may cause financial distress later so be careful.

Health

The period is set to begin on a positive note, with Jupiter in Lagna providing you with strength and confidence. You will feel fresh and optimistic about the upcoming period. Your friends will be a source of constant love and support. Your analytical mind will help you make rational decisions and see beyond outer appearances, guiding you toward the right path and fostering a healthy lifestyle. However, as the year progresses, you will take on new responsibilities, leading to extra hours of work, lack of sleep, and excessive stress, which may take a toll on your health. There will be a tendency to gain weight during this entire period.

After 14 May 2025, it's important to pay attention to your health as Jupiter will transit to the second house and aspect the eighth house, potentially leading to medical expenditures. Digestive and stomach-related issues might arise, and recovery could take time. From 13 July to 28 Nov 2025, there may be medical issues related to legs, knees, and feet, especially for individuals with afflicted Saturn in their birth chart. They should be particularly cautious about their legs during that period. To maintain good health, it is advised to adopt a routine of regular walking, jogging, or running, which will keep Saturn happy and minimize health issues. Saturn will be closely monitoring your health for a significant part of the year, and if you lead a sedentary lifestyle without exercise, it might lead to health issues.

With Jupiter in the second house, be mindful of your diet as it may increase, leading to potential weight-related health issues. Fasting on

Thursdays or a day of your choice can be beneficial for health-related matters. Making significant changes in your eating habits, along with regular exercise and weekly fasting, can improve your overall well-being. Health should be a top priority, so ensure you follow through with medical check-ups as advised and stay proactive about your health.

Love Life and Marriage

With the onset of year 2025, Jupiter aspects from the Lagna (first house) to the fifth, seventh, and ninth houses bode well for love relationships, marriage, and overall luck. This is a promising time to potentially meet your soul mate, the person you've been seeking. If the timing aligns, marriage may be on the horizon, and it is advisable for those already in a relationship to consider getting married during this period. The period is quite positive and there are chances that unmarried people searching for soul mates may get married.

However, after 14 May 2025, Jupiter transits to the second house, which is considered the "marka" house, implying it may not be as beneficial for married life, especially for females. Jupiter's positioning in the eighth position from the second house, the natural significator of marriage for females, could lead to challenges in married life for some individuals. The period from 15 Sep to 09 Oct 2025, when Ketu conjuncts with Venus in the Leo sign, is particularly highlighted as a potentially difficult time. Extra care and attention are needed during this period to navigate any challenges that may arise.

The period 18 Oct to 11 Nov 2025 again is positive and holds the potential for significant changes in love matters and marriage. Jupiter aspects from the third house to the seventh, and ninth houses bode well for love relationships, marriage, and overall luck. This is a promising time to potentially meet your soul mate, the person you've been seeking. If the timing aligns, marriage may be on the horizon, and it is advisable for those already in a relationship to consider getting married during this period.

I will advise to unmarried that now not to delay their marriage proposals as mentioned above as Jupiter in the second house will not be in a supporting role. You need to have very strong Yogas to get married during the period when Jupiter transits in the second house.

For married people, the period between 14 May to 18 Oct 2025, you may find some suffocation in your love relations. That may be due to the reason that you have started having big plans and you find your love relations are not matching your expectations, so you trying to avoid meeting them. Take your time and don't rush into matters of love. Building a stable relationship requires careful analysis of the person you are interested in. Saturn's aspect on the fifth house puts caution and delays in the love affairs. Romance should unfold naturally; avoid trying to force it, as it may only create distance between you and your partner. Instead, focus on communication and understanding each other's personal space.

Progeny

For Taurus natives, the period before 14 May 2025 is good in matters of progeny. The period after 18 Oct to 05 Dec 2025 will also be quite positive.

Education

Period till 14 May 2025, Jupiter aspect on the fifth house has given a lot of support on the educational front. You will get the results after hard work because Ketu diverts you and you need to remain focussed. Those who are looking to go abroad for higher education may find a positive period. Rahu transit in the eleventh house provides an opportunity for students to go abroad for higher education. After 18 May 2025, Ketu will transit to the fourth house and the fifth house will be free from any affliction. Due to the aspect of Saturn, things may get delayed but are assured. Students have to work harder as Saturn will restrict or delay but will ensure that those who are worthy, hardworking and righteous will still benefit in the end.

Spiritualism

As Jupiter will transit in the Lagna, you may have a strong desire for spiritual growth and a quest for higher understanding. You may be attracted to spiritual practices and may have deep insights into spiritual matters. You may develop certain psychic abilities or have an interest in the occult.

However, after 14 May 2025, Jupiter transit to the second house and aspect the eighth house. You may be led to delusions or a distorted understanding of spirituality. You need to keep a balance and not get carried away by your spiritual pursuits, as this can lead to problems in other areas of your life. You may be drawn to unhealthy or unwise spiritual practices or beliefs, or to become too focused on material gains and pleasure at the expense of your spiritual development. You may have to struggle with issues related to your subconscious mind and your past actions. They may also face challenges in their spiritual pursuits and may be prone to illusion and delusion. You may lose your interest in spirituality as expenses and health may be issues of concern. You may be more focused on making money and stop doing charity or donation.

MONTH WISE PREDICTIONS

After going through predictions in general, let us find out certain periods where some changes will be expected. I wanted to use the calendar month but that may not be functional as it will not follow any pattern of movement of any planet. Sun transit sign after 30 days and that date falls on 14 to 17 of any month. Moon transits a sign after 2.25 days. Sun being the life force and largest planet has the maximum effect on human life and affairs. So, I will be using the transit of the Sun, which takes 30 days and then include the transit of other planets, during that period. Considering the effect of conjunctions of planets during that period further helps to reach better accuracy. Major Planets such as Saturn, Rahu, Ketu and Jupiter are going to transit for longer durations and affect the life path in the long term. But within that large span, good or bad events will occur based on the transit of inner planets. I could only think of this as the best option. Your comments or feedback on this is always welcome to improve the procedures.

You should consider that these predictions are based on general planetary movement and do not consider the natal chart of individuals. Period, sub-period and planet position in the natal chart have major significance and vary from person to person. It is better to consult an astrologer for a personalised annual horoscope. It does not cost much but gives you some psychological support and some warning for which you can take some precautions. Also, remember that there is no remedy for fixed or incurable Karmas as you have to face them in this life cycle or the next one.

Period: 01 Jan to 13 Jan 2025

The planetary position on 01 Jan 2025, as Sun is in transit in Sagittarius, the planetary position for the Taurus sign will be as per the chart: -

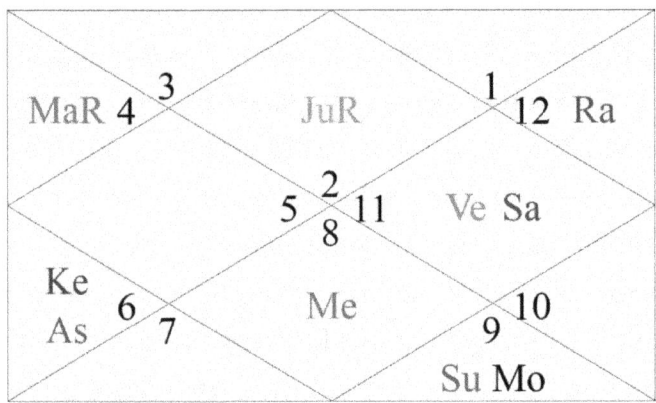

During this period, retrograde Mercury will turn to direct on 16 Dec 2024 and transit to Sagittarius on 4 Jan 2025, Jupiter as has been retrograde since 09 Oct 2024 in Taurus sign will continue to be retrograde till 04 Feb 2025. Mars has been in retrograde motion in Cancer since 7 Dec 2024 and will continue in retrograde motion.

Venus will be in conjunction with Saturn in the Aquarius sign from 28 Dec 2024 to 28 Jan 2025.

Sun transit in the eighth house, weak Mars in the third house till 21 Jan 2025 and Retro Jupiter in Lagna till 04 Feb 2025, may bring some health issues. There could be a noticeable depletion of life force and energy due to health concerns affecting you or your family members, especially the parents of your or yours's life partner. This might necessitate visits to the hospital to care for your loved ones and manage associated expenses.

You may become an introvert and would like to analyse the decisions taken in the past. It's a time for introspection and understanding your desires, fears, and motivations. it can signify a time of significant inner growth and personal evolution. It may bring to the surface issues related to power dynamics, psychological depth, and issues of control.

You may be linked to the mystical, occult, and esoteric subjects and find yourself drawn to such matters or have experiences that encourage you to explore these realms. You may be facing fears and embracing transformation.

There may be many financial ups and downs during this period. There can be major disputes regarding inheritance, insurance or some commission due. You may be faced with some issues of dispute with your siblings or father. You may not get the support of the government, power, authority or even his seniors.

Rahu is in transit in the Pisces sign in the 11th house since 30 Oct 2023 and will continue to transit till 18 May 2025. Being In the eleventh house, which is the house of gains and social networking, you will continue to have a lot of positivity and support from social circles, friends and groups. You will make unconventional efforts to grow in business. However, that unconventional approach during this period may land you in trouble so be cautious of doing any mischief action till 04 Feb 2025

Rahu and Jupiter aspect on the seventh house indicates that those who are married may find some issues of lack of trust or faith amongst each other and may get into a disagreement. This is the time to relax and avoid any unnecessary disputes.

Due to ongoing vacation moods or holiday trips, the attention to the education side is generally lost. Students should focus on their studies. You cannot change the subjects now. Taking a break for one year for studies may be an idea emerging in mind, that needs to be reconsidered.

For those who are expecting progeny, I advise them to consult the Doctor regularly.

Period: 14 Jan to 12 Feb 2025

The planetary position as the Sun transit to the Capricorn sign will be as under:-

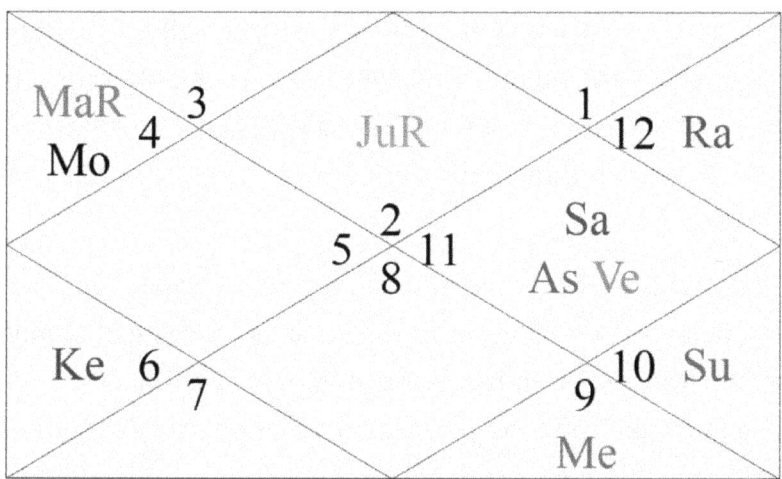

During this period, Mars in retrograde movement transits to Gemini on 21 Jan 2025, Mercury transits to Capricorn on 24 Jan 2025, Venus transits in Pisces on 28 Jan 2025 till 31 May 2025 and then Mercury shifts to Aquarius on 11 Feb 2025. Jupiter became direct on 04 Feb 2025.

Conjunction of planets, Venus and Saturn in Aquarius from 28 Dec to 28 Jan 2025, Sun and Mercury in Capricorn from 24 Jan to 11 Feb 2025. Venus and Rahu in Pisces from 28 Jan to 31 May 2025.

During this period, the Sun will be in transit in the ninth house, the house of religion, morality, higher education and father. Your focus area will be your parents, long travels, religious activities, legal issues and even health issues of self or parents. You may be required to travel a lot for business or adventure activities. If you're involved in the touring job, you may be required to visit long distances or even foreign places. I find these tours or visits may not be conducive as fruitful as per your expectations.

During this period, you can expect a lot of positivity and numerous opportunities coming your way. Your confidence will soar, and you'll feel more optimistic about life. This positive outlook will make you eager to take on challenges and go after your goals. Those in politics or position of power and authority may find the period quite positive for them. You may experience an increase in social activities and conversations with those around you.

You will remain energetic during this period. You might feel motivated to study new subjects or engage in activities that stimulate your intellectual curiosity or impart your higher education. Your pursuit of spiritual matters and philosophical contemplation may lead you to travel and meet some religious people.

You will get happiness from brothers and sisters and even your children, however over expectations from them may lead to stress. The health of siblings may be an issue of concern for you However, you need to avoid arrogance with the seniors and your father. Your stubbornness and aggressive attitude can land you in antagonising the elders and superiors.

Due to Venus Rahu conjunction in the eleventh house from 28 Jan to 31 May 2025, you need to be cautious about your relationship. You may support or get support from your friends or social group. You may be crowded with friends of opposite sex and the relationship with them may be quite trendy and fluctuating.

Period: 13 Feb to 14 Mar 2025

The planetary position for Taurus sign, when Sun transit to Aquarius will be as under:-

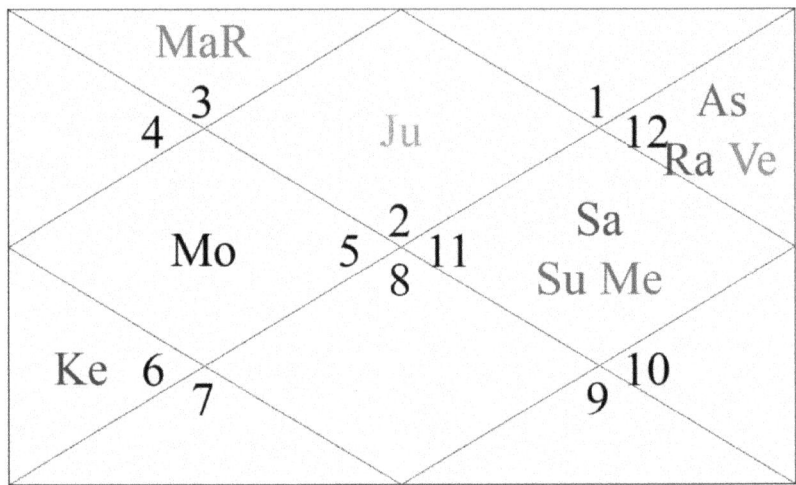

During this period, Mars will become direct on 24 Feb 2025 in Gemini. Mercury transits to Pisces on 27 Feb 2025. Venus will become retrograde in Pisces from 2 Mar 2025 to 13 Apr 2025.

Conjunction In Pisces sign, Rahu conjunct with Venus in Pisces from 28 Jan to 27 Feb 2025. In Aquarius, Saturn and Mercury conjunct from 11 Feb to 12 Feb 2025, Saturn, Mercury and Sun from 12 Feb to 27 Feb 2025 and then Saturn and Sun from 27 Feb to 14 Mar 2025.

Sun transit in the tenth house, house of profession is poised to bring positive transformations in one's professional life. However here the transit is over the Saturn which restricts the gains which one can achieve. Individually Sun and Saturn both give excellent results in tenth house however their conjunction tries to restrict those or delay the outcome.

Despite high level of confidence and positive outlook about life, you may face challenges at health and professional level. There can be last minute delay or obstacle in the individual earning acclaim, prominence, and acknowledgment. You have to work harder to achieve the desired results. I do not find appropriate at this time to change the job. During this period, you will remain connected to your professional activities. Remember that tenth houses is house of Karmas and you have to work hard. Success will not come automatically but if you make an effort, you will be victorious despite the obstacles.

Sun and Saturn conjunction is being formed in the Aquarius sign which is again a sign of social networking. Sun and Saturn are the extremes of the Solar system where the Sun represents the life force and Saturn signifies the end-of-life force. One radiates the energy and the other absorbs the entire energy as a black body. A similar effect can be observed here during this period, where you may have a contrast in requirements regarding health and Job pressure. You may not get the requisite support from the higher authorities or government. There may be a clash of ego with the higher-ups. There may be differences of opinion to extreme levels with the higher authorities, government officials and even your father. Relations with your father or the health of father may be an issue of concern for you. Those having a period or sub period of Sun or Saturn may face some form of humiliation or allegation.

You may not be satisfied with the achievements of your children especially after 28 Feb 2025. I suppose exam pressure or worry about their academic performance which may not be as per your expectations causing stressful relations.

There might also be a desire to control and get involved in activities at home front or family. You may try to explore and understand your emotional needs and seek comfort and security within your family and close relationships. There may be some family function family reunion or some auspicious activity.

I do not recommend any major decision regarding the purchase of property or shifting of jobs as Mars will be in retrograde motion till 24 Feb 2024. Despite your best efforts at the professional level, you have to struggle on all fronts.

Venus in retro motion will be conjunct with Rahu from 2 Mar to 13 Apr 2025. During this period, person may have issues in married life or regarding health of life partner. Be careful regarding trust issues within love relationship. The recent friendship with opposite sex which have not been tested in times may not continue.

Period: 15 Mar to 13 Apr 2025

The planetary position for Taurus Sign as on 15 Mar 2025 will be as under:-

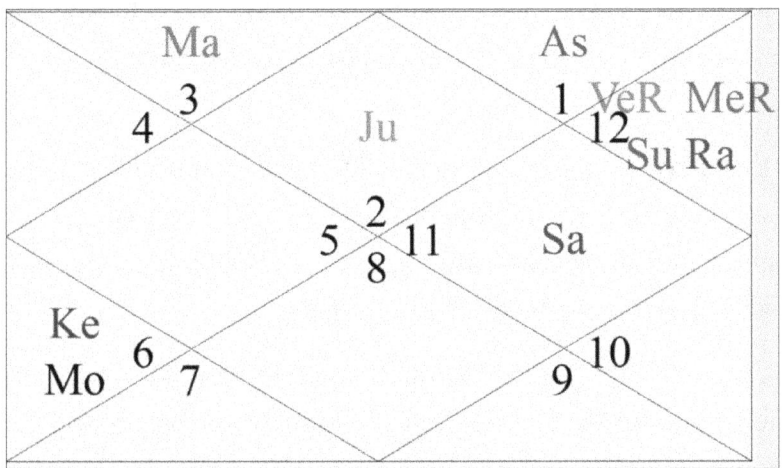

During this period, a major transit of Saturn is happening when Saturn transits to Pisces on 29 Mar 2025 for a period of 2 years 2 months till 3 June 2027. This is a major transit when Sade Sati of Aries will commence and Capricorn will be free from Shani Sade Sati. Mercury will be in retro in Pisces from 15 Mar to 07 Apr 2025. Mars will enter Cancer on 3 Apr 2025 till 7 June 2025. Venus will be direct in Pisces on 13 Apr 2025. Rahu transit to Aquarius and Ketu to Leo on 18 May 2025.

Conjunction, In Pisces, Rahu Venus, Mercury and Sun conjunct from 14 Mar to 29 Mar 2025. **After Saturn transit to Pisces on 29 Mar 2025, five planets Rahu, Saturn, Mercury, Venus and Sun will be in conjunction from 29 Mar to 14 Apr 2025. Kaal Sarp Yoga is being formed on 29 Mar 2025.**

During this period, Sun will be in transit in the eleventh house, house of gains and social networking. You will be ambitious and aggressive in your professional life but still tend to have a vast and diverse social network. You will be outwardly, friendly, outgoing, and enjoy being part of various groups and communities. People will be drawn towards you due to your charismatic and confident personality. You will have ambitious goals and dreams which you want to achieve. Though to achieve success you have to work hard and also remain grounded and humble.

You may get a leadership role in social or professional groups and can be a motivating factor for others. You will continue to be inclined towards humanitarian causes and your activities may actively contribute to society and work for the betterment of others.

You will be able to make some wise decisions regarding investment. You will get name, fame, income from various sources, favour from friends and will enjoy good health. There may be opposition from your friend circle but still you will emerge as victorious and gain popularity. Your friend circle will increase. Those who are in social media may find that their follower base has improved a lot during this period. You may get a rise in income, status and your powers.

You will have a strong sense for recognition and will be recognised by participating in social activities, events, and gatherings. Your contribution to society or hard work in professional life may attracts others to You.

On 29 Mar 2025, Saturn joins the Rahu Sun, Mercury, Venus's conjunction. A Kaal Sarp yoga is being formed. Those who are in public domain and not having transparent dealing may be implicated with charges of corruption or malpractice. Certain issues may emerge related to the health and even on professional front. Health of father or some near one may result in visit to hospitals and heavy expenditure.

Rahu positioned here occults the Sun and create a false ego. This false ego may result in making wrong decisions which may be quite problematic at a later stage.

Mercury turns retrograde from 15 Mar to 07 Apr 2025 so be cautious while making any major decisions related to the family activities, marriage and investment.

I find the period of Kaal Sarp, 29 Mar to 13 Sep 2025. All the planets except Moon will be in the grip of Rahu and Ketu. This period will be quite sensitive period which may find number of untoward incidences worldwide.

Period: 14 Apr to 14 May 2025

The planetary position for the Taurus Sign as on 14 Mar 2025 will be as under: -

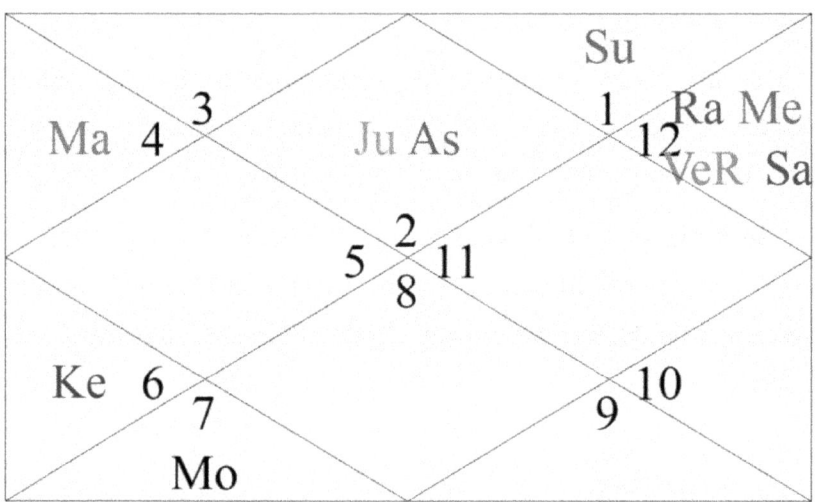

During this period, Mercury transit to Aries on 7 May 2025, Jupiter transit to Gemini on 14 May 2025.

Conjunction In Pisces, Rahu, Saturn, Mercury and Venus conjunct from 14 Apr to 07 May 2025. Rahu, Saturn and Venus from 7 May to 18 May 2025. In Aries, Sun and Mercury from 7 May to 15 May 2025

During this period, Sun will transit in the twelfth house, in the Aries sign which is its exaltation sign.

During this period, you may have look for deeper meaning in life and explore the realms of the subconscious and spirituality. You may have a tendency towards introspection and privacy and would like to spend time alone. You may also experience a sense of isolation or feeling different from others. This is the time you might have time to undiscover skills that could emerge with self-discovery and exploration. You may be travelling to a spiritual place or explore spiritual journey during this period. You will tend to be compassionate, empathetic, and understanding towards others' struggles and pain.

Sun will provide you good results in terms of health as you may recover from health issues, if any. You may gain from foreign contacts or people involved in spiritual practices or pharma sector. If some one if looking to travel or settle abroad, he may get an opportunity. You may also get an opportunity to travel abroad for an official work or for leisure. Your employer may like to send you to negotiate a deal with any client.

Mars will be in transit in the third house from 03 Apr to 07 June 2025. Mars being in debilitation in the third house make cause you to lose its strength, courage and fighting capability. You may often show courage and anger in wrong circumstances and lack initiatives. You may plan a lot but will not be having initiative to start action. There may be some issues concerning your siblings as his health or progress in life may be affected. You may have some communication issues due to your emotional outburst.

Period: 15 May to 14 June 2025

The planetary position for Taurus at the time Sun transit to Taurus will be as per chart: -

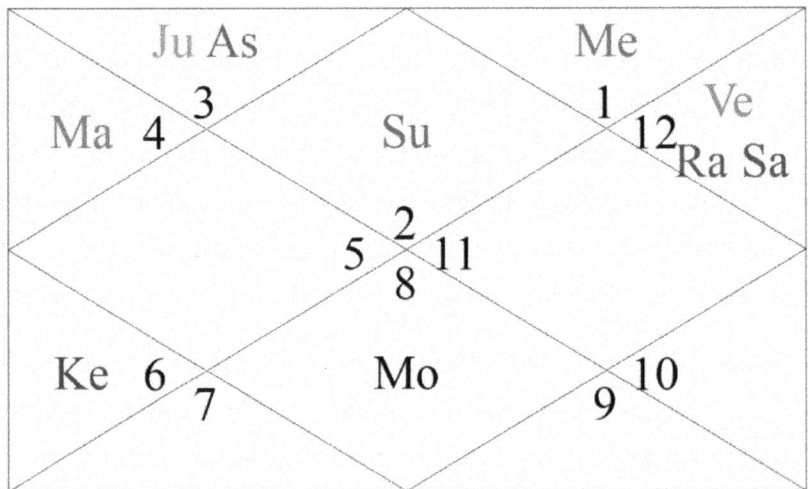

During the upcoming period, Jupiter transit to Gemini on 14 May 2025, Rahu transit to Aquarius and Ketu in Leo on 18 May 2025, Mercury in Taurus on 23 May 2025, Venus will enter in Gemini on 06 June 2025. Mercury transit to Gemini on 6 June 2025, Mars enters Leo on 7 June 2025.

Conjunction In Pisces, Rahu, Saturn and Venus from 7 May to 18 May 205, Venus and Saturn from 18 May to 31 May 2025. In Taurus, Sun and Mercury conjunct from 23 May to 6 June 2025. In Gemini, Jupiter and Mercury conjunct from 6 June to 15 June 2025. In Leo sign, Ketu and Mars conjunct from 7 June to 28 July 2025.

During this period, Sun transit in Lagna and you can expect a lot of positivity and numerous opportunities coming your way. Your confidence will soar, and you'll feel more optimistic about life. This positive outlook will make you eager to take on challenges and go after your goals. New opportunities will open, leading to growth in various aspects of your life. Your efforts may be recognized, and you could see success in your endeavours. People around you will look up to you for guidance and inspiration, and you might find yourself leading important projects.

During this period, your primary emphasis will be on self-health, self-growth, matters related to relationships, partnerships, marriage, and one-to-one connections. You're expected to consider your significant relationships, including those with your spouse, romantic partner, or close business associates. You might feel more assertive in your relationships and express your individuality within the context of your partnerships This attitude of yours could create some challenges or conflicts with your life partner or business partner.

You will be ambitious and will have courage to express yourself and lead others. You would like to explore and broaden your horizons. You could achieve significant milestones and make progress toward your long-term goals. This newfound self-assurance will contribute to your overall well-being and success.

Due to your busy schedule or ego issues, your interests towards sexual interest will be lacking which further may affect your relationship with your life partner. Sun is a separatist planet and its aspect over the seventh house creates a lot of ego and anger issues resulting in disagreement with the life partner.

Period from 07 June 2025 to 28 July 2025, Mars will be in transit in the fourth house in conjunction with Ketu and aspected by Rahu. It is advisable to steer clear of property-related dealings during this period.

You need to be attentive towards health issues of self and your parents. Avoid anger and ego issues at home as they may be the cause of disputes at home. Parental property disputes may come up during this transit. Better to wait rather than look for a resolution during this period. Due to anger issues or desire to dominate the family members, one can create a rift between two. Be submissive and avoid arrogance.

Period: 15 June to 15 July 2025

The planetary position for Taurus sign at the time Sun transit to Gemini will be as per chart: -

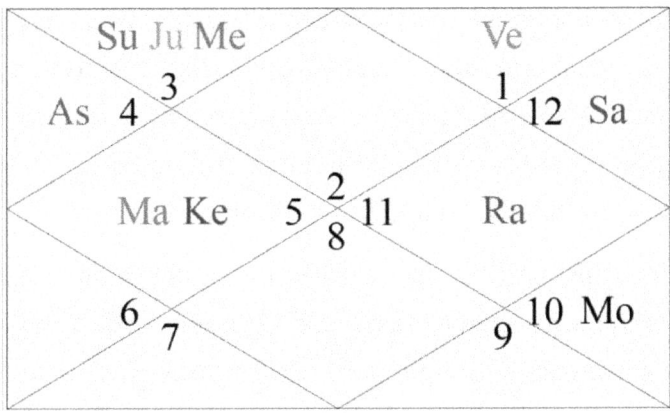

During this period, Mercury will enter Cancer on 22 June 2025, Venus enter Taurus on 29 June 2025. Saturn is going to be retrograde on 13 Jul 2025 in Pisces Sign. This retrogradation of 139 days is likely to affect all the signs and specially signs which are aspected by Saturn.

Conjunction In Leo sign, Ketu and Mars conjunct from 7 June to 28 July 2025. In Gemini, Jupiter and Venus conjunct from 26 Jul to 21 Aug 2025.

Sun transit in second house, house of speech, family and finances will create lot of opportunities or challenges regarding financial matters, such as inheritance, loans, debts, or joint ventures. Your communication skills will be appreciated by others and you will prove yourself as an eloquent speaker. You will get an opportunity to interact with your family members. Any of your family member may get an appreciation or recognition. There may be growth in family or some family function for which you will be playing a major role as a responsible family member or as a sponsor for the function.

This period can bring financial opportunities and potential growth in income and resources. It may be a favourable time for financial matters and investments. You will have optimism and confidence in handling financial matters and making wise decisions related to money. You will be inclined to be generous and engage in charitable activities, supporting others in need. You may enhance self-expression, leading to effective communication regarding financial matters and personal values. You will have a positive attitude and a hopeful outlook on life.

During this period, you will enjoy good health, happiness and increase in popularity, name, fame and reputation. You may get income from various sources. Though your expenditure will also increase for medical, foreign travels, luxuries. If you are looking for a loan, you may get the same easily.

Saturn retrogradation from 13 July 2025 is likely to affect your relationship. Gains that you were expecting may not fructify easily or get delayed. You may find some health issues or pains reemerge, if the dietary habits are not modified.

Period: 16 July to 16 Aug 2025

The planetary position for Taurus sign at the time Sun transit to Cancer will be as per chart: -

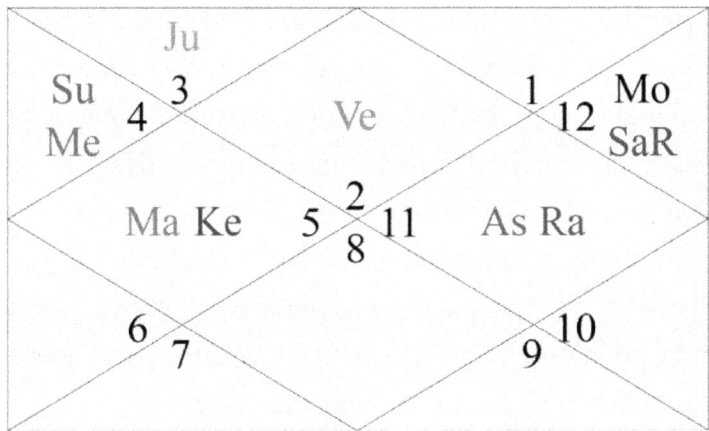

In this forthcoming period, Mercury become retrograde from 18 July to 11 Aug 2025, Venus transit to Gemini on 26 July 2025 and Mars transit to Virgo on 28 July 2025.

Conjunction In Cancer, Sun and Mercury conjunct from 16 Jul to 17 Aug 2025. In Gemini, Jupiter and Venus conjunct from 26 Jul to 21 Aug 2025

During this period, you will be full of energy, initiative, ego and desire to dominate. Sun transit in the third house, an upachay house, house of communication and siblings brings the best of the time for the native. You can expect a lot of positivity and numerous opportunities coming your way. Your confidence will soar, and you'll feel more optimistic about life. This positive outlook will make you eager to take on challenges and go after your goals. New opportunities will open, leading to growth in various aspects of your life. Your efforts may be recognized, and you could see success in your endeavours. People around you will look up to you for guidance and inspiration, and you might find yourself leading important projects.

The period seems promising with positive prospects in various aspects of your life. There may be gains in income, rise in position, overall happiness, recovery from disease and success in new ventures. This period is associated with recognition by superiors, promotion and appreciation of the job. Your focus area will be your profession, colleagues, short travels, and communications. You may feel more decisive and able to make quick decisions, especially concerning everyday matters. It's a good time for reconnecting and resolving any communication issues. However, there may be some trouble getting along with your family members, especially your siblings which may be due to your ego issues.

However, due to the Mars Ketu conjunction from 07 June to 28 July 2025, you should be careful about excessive anger and initiative. Due to anger issues or desire to dominate the love one can create a rift between two. Be submissive and avoid arrogance.

You need to be cautious after 18 July 2025, while signing any legal documents. You may find that you are not able to decide matter related to property. Renovation or dealing with the property may keep your mind in confusion. You get in a dilemma about how to react in family and social relationships.

, At the professional level, the period will give positive results however at family happiness something will be missing.

Period: 17 Aug to 16 Sep 2025

The planetary position for the Taurus sign at the time Sun transit to Leo will be as per the chart: -

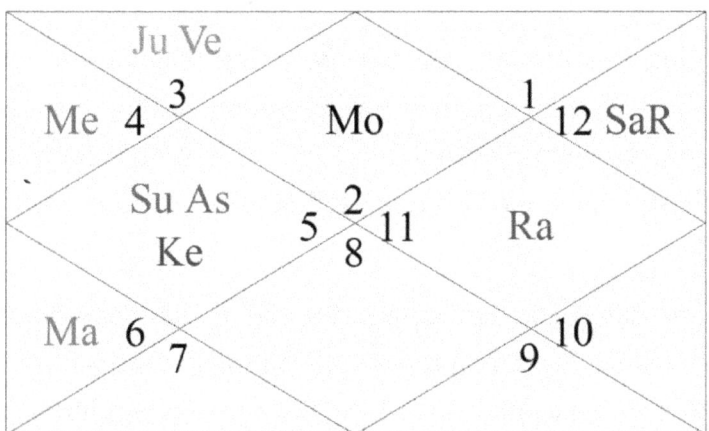

During this period, Venus transit to Cancer on 21 Aug 2025, Mercury to Leo on 30 Aug 2025, Mars in Libra on 13 Sep 2025 and Mercury in Virgo on 15 Sep 2025.

Conjunction In Leo, Ketu and Sun from 17 Aug to 30 Aug 2025. In Cancer, Mercury and Venus from 21 Aug to 30 Aug 2025. In Gemini, Jupiter and Venus conjunct from 26 Jul to 21 Aug 2025

During this period, the Sun will transit in the fourth house which is the house of mother, comforts and luxuries of life, emotions and soft feelings. you will remain connected to your family members and home life. There might be a desire to spend more time at home or to engage in activities that involve your family.

This is a favourable time for home-related activities, such as renovating, redecorating, or making changes to your living space to enhance your comfort and well-being. There may be some family function or family reunion or some auspicious activity. You may like to visit your hometown or your ancestral place or temple. You might feel more inclined to explore your family history and heritage and would like to nurture and support others, especially your family members and loved ones.

During this period, you will be doing well in your professional domain. You will get support from the seniors and the government. You may find a new contract or crack a deal that will be appreciated by your seniors. Those who want to buy or sell land or property may succeed in this period.

Avoid anger and ego issues at home as they may be the cause of disputes at home. Parental property disputes may come up during this transit. Better to wait rather than look for a resolution during this period. Due to anger issues or desire to dominate the love one can create a rift between two. Be submissive and avoid arrogance. Take care of your health regarding the digestion part. Medical attention may be required during this period.

Period: 17 Sep to 17 Oct 2025

The planetary position for the Taurus sign at the time Sun transit to Virgo will be as per the chart: -

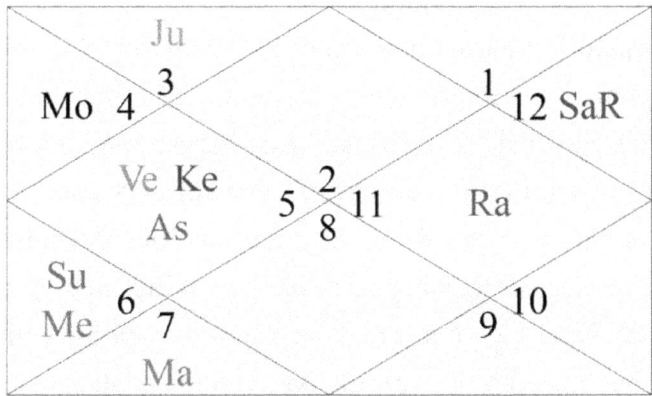

During the period, Mercury transit to Libra on 3 Oct 2025, Venus in Virgo on 3 Oct 2025.

Conjunction In Leo, Ketu, Sun and Venus conjunct from 15 Sep to 17 Sep 2025, Ketu and Venus from 17 Sep to 9 Oct 2025. In Virgo, Sun and Mercury from 17 Sep to 3 Oct 2025, Sun and Venus from 9 Oct to 17 Oct 2025

During this period, the Sun will be in transit in the fifth house of the chart. The fifth house is the house of creativity, education and progeny and also the repository of past life deeds. This will bring good results in terms of education, love relations, speculations, progeny, creative pursuits and happiness. This period will be a mix of your priorities regarding success and social networking. You may connect both and can have major gains in your profession. This is a positive time for progeny, education, career success, leadership, and positive social interactions. You will be ambitious and aggressive in your professional life but still tend to have a vast and diverse social network. You will be friendly, outgoing, and enjoy being part of various groups and communities. You may find time to engage in artistic or expressive activities, pursuing hobbies, artistic endeavours, and activities that bring joy. This may be due to the reason that during the adverse conditions on other fronts, you want to keep yourself occupied in your own world or get involved in activities that give you some relief. You might seek entertainment, engage in recreational activities, or attend social events that bring happiness. You may feel more adventurous and willing to step out of your comfort zone to pursue your passions. You may even go for an adventurous hike during this period. If you have a flair for performing or public speaking, then you may get an opportunity to showcase your talents and that may boost your confidence. You might be engaged in speculative ventures, such as investing or gambling. It's essential to exercise caution and not take excessive risks during this transit. You could get involved in spending time with children, being more involved in their lives, or considering matters related to parenting.

For some individuals, this transit might be related to matters of fertility, conception, or pregnancy. For students, this period can be quite positive and those who are looking to go abroad for higher studies may find success, but they will be struggling a lot for Visa.

There can be damage to some luxury items such as Vehicle, mobile or computer. The health of your life partner or your relationship with her can be an issue of concern.

Period: 18 Oct to 16 Nov 2025

The planetary position for Taurus at the time Sun transit to Libra will be as per the chart: -

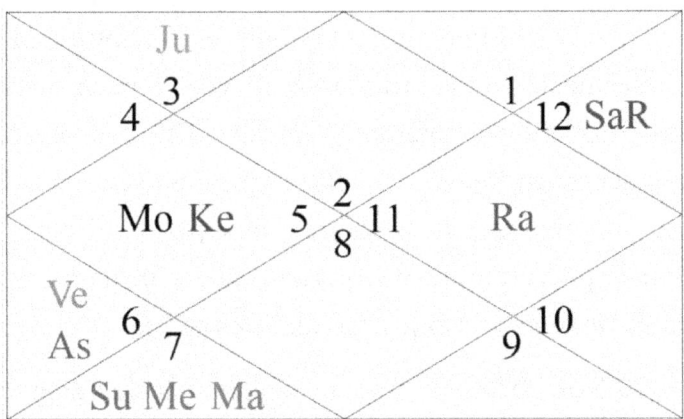

During this period, Jupiter transit to Cancer on 18 Oct 2025, Mercury in Scorpio on 24 Oct 2025, Mars in Scorpio on 27 Oct 2025. On 10 Nov 2025, Mercury become retrograde in Scorpio and then on 11 Nov 2025, Jupiter become retrograde in Cancer.

Conjunction In Scorpio, Mars and Mercury from 27 Oct to 16 Nov 2025.

This period can be quite positive as the Sun, Mars and Mercury in the sixth house ensures your victory over enemies. Long pending issues, disputes or debts can be resolved by your intelligence, initiative and communication. You will have success in financial matters. Those who are appearing in competitions may be successful. During this time, you could be quite busy with your work and managing your daily routine and responsibilities. Any health issues if troubling for long or since last month may be cured. You will be bestowed with good health, good earnings and success in new ventures. You may get involved with charitable activities. This is a good time to focus on personal growth and becoming better at various aspects of your life. You may get the chance to showcase your leadership qualities by participating in important meetings, making crucial decisions, and guiding others. As a result, your public image and reputation are likely to improve, and people will admire and respect you for your achievements and contributions. If you've been seeking new job opportunities, promotions, upgrades, or rewards, this period holds the potential for success in these areas. If any promotions, rewards or awards are pending, you will get them during this period. Your rapport with superiors will improve during this period. You will gain confidence, get success in new ventures and enjoy the luxuries of life.

After 10 Nov 2025, you find the situation is changing and you have to work harder. Your good nature and inbuilt mechanism to help others is resulting in yourself getting involved in conflict management of others. Despite your efforts at work, you may not receive the recognition you deserve. You might also find yourself dealing with and resolving conflicts or problems that come up at work or in your daily life. During this period, practical tasks and responsibilities will require your attention. Find a balance between a helpful nature and your professional requirements.

On the family front, Venus Ketu conjunction and Mars in the seventh house is not quite positive and the native may find problems in love relations or with his life partner. The reason will be an ego clash or loss of trust in each other due to elevated sexual desires. The health of life partner or family members may be an issue of concern. The family issues may trigger a sense of isolation at the family front.

Period: 17 Nov to 15 Dec 2025

The planetary position for the Taurus sign at the time Sun transit to Scorpio will be as per the chart:-

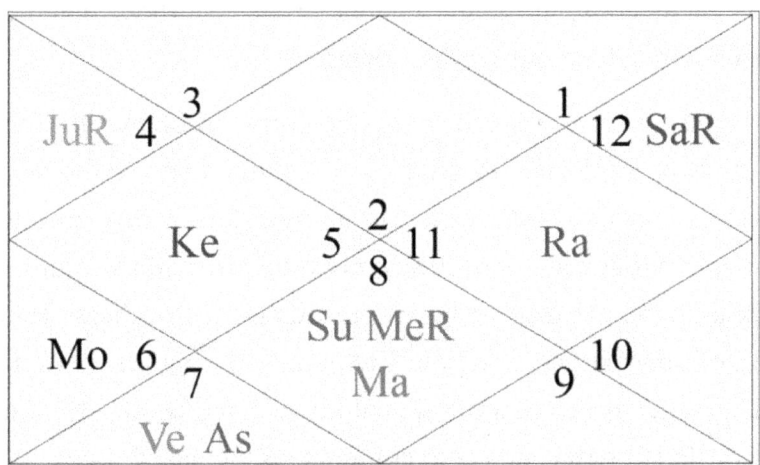

During this period, Mercury transit to Libra on 23 Nov 2025 in retro movement, Venus in Scorpio on 26 Nov 2025. Saturn becomes direct on 28 Nov 2025 in Pisces. Mercury becomes direct in Libra on 29 Nov 2025 and then enters Scorpio on 16 Dec 2025.

Conjunction In Scorpio, Mars and Mercury conjunct from 27 Oct to 16 Nov 2025. Sun joins this conjunction from 16 Oct 2025, On 23 Nov 2023, Mercury is out of conjunction from 23 Nov to 6 Dec 20525 due to its retro movement to Libra. Venus Joins this conjunction on 26 Nov 2025. On 7 Dec 2025, Mars will transit to the next sign and the conjunction of Sun, Mercury and Venus continue till 16 Dec 2025. Mercury and Venus conjunct from 16 Dec to 20 Dec 2025 in Scorpio.

During this time, your focus will be on relationships, partnerships, marriage, and one-on-one connections. You'll likely pay more attention to your significant relationships, such as with your spouse, romantic partner, or close business associates. There will be increased interactions and activities with them. You might feel more assertive in your relationships and express your individuality within the context of your partnerships. However, there could be some challenges or conflicts that need to be addressed and resolved during this period.

If you are married, there may be some problems in your married life till 26 Nov 2025. It's advised to be cautious and avoid unnecessary arguments or conflicts with your life partner during this time to prevent any trouble. Your social connections might be affected by your attitude, so it's essential to be mindful of how you interact with others. Take care of the health of your parents and your life partner during this period. After 26 Nov 2025, Venus transits to the seventh house and positivity in the affairs of married life is observed. There could be an increased focus on romantic interactions, and you may feel more playful and spontaneous in your relationships. You could get involved in spending time with family and being more involved in their lives.

Legal matters or negotiations with others may come into the picture more prominently, but the outcomes may not always align with your desires. It's crucial to find a balance between asserting your independence and the need for cooperation and compromise in your partnerships.

On the professional front and for your social status, you may grow and can have major gains in your profession. This is a positive time for career success, leadership, and positive social interactions. You will be ambitious and aggressive in your professional life but still tend to have a vast and diverse social network. You will be friendly, outgoing, and enjoy being part of various groups and communities. People will be drawn towards you due to your charismatic and confident personality. You will have ambitious goals and dreams which you want to achieve. Though to achieve success you must work hard and also remain grounded and humble.

You may get a leadership role in social or professional groups and can be a motivating factor for others. You will tend to be involved in generosity and humanitarian causes and your activities may actively contribute to society and work for the betterment of others.

Period: 16 Dec to 31 Dec 2025

The planetary position for the Taurus sign at the time Sun transit to Scorpio will be as per the chart:-

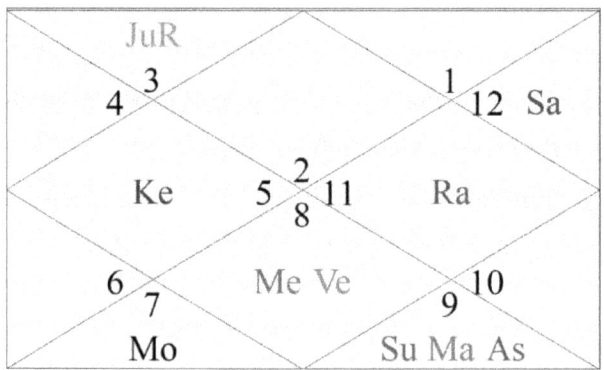

During this period, Venus transits to Sagittarius on 16 Dec 2025, Mercury transit to Sagittarius on 29 Dec 2025.

Conjunction, Mercury and Venus conjunct from 16 Dec to 20 Dec 2025 in Scorpio. In Sagittarius, Sun and Mars conjunct from 16 Dec to 20 Dec 2025, Sun, Mars and Venus from 20 Dec to 29 Dec 2025, Sun, Mars, Mercury and Venus from 25 Dec 2025 to 13 Jan 2026.

Sun and Mars transit in the eighth house may bring some health issues or accidents. There could be a noticeable depletion of life force and energy due to health concerns affecting you or your family members, especially the parents of your or yours's life partner. This might necessitate visits to the hospital to care for your loved ones and manage associated expenses. The aspect of Jupiter is the saving grace and may provide major relief and help you with all problems. You can also consider that in times of crisis, guidance or help from some of your elder family members will be your savior.

You may become an introvert and would like to analyse the decisions taken in the past. It's a time for introspection and understanding your desires, fears, and motivations. it can signify a time of significant inner growth and personal evolution. It may bring to the surface issues related to power dynamics, psychological depth, and issues of control.

You may be linked to the mystical, occult, and esoteric subjects and find yourself drawn to such matters or have experiences that encourage you to explore these realms.

During this period, you may be faced with opportunities or challenges regarding financial matters, such as inheritance, loans, debts, or joint ventures. Investments in stocks or mutual funds may be in a negative zone and you need to wait rather than get in a panic.

REMEDIES FOR TAURUS

For individuals born under the sign of Taurus, Saturn holds a significant role as the Yoga Karak planet, governing the ninth and tenth houses. A strong Saturn in the Taurus chart has the potential to bestow success, robust health, favourable fortune and a strong professional arena upon the native. However, if you encounter issues related to knees, legs, Vata imbalances, hair loss, or frequent turnover of servants or employees, it signifies an afflicted and inauspicious Saturn.

To alleviate this situation, several measures can be taken. Regular walks, increased protein intake, maintaining humility, and avoiding the colour black are recommended to pacify Saturn. Additionally, if Saturn is not positioned in the sixth, eighth, or twelfth house, wearing a black sapphire or its substitute in the middle finger of the right hand is advisable. Wearing a black thread on the right ankle or an iron ring on the middle finger of the right hand may also give some help. Engaging in acts of charity and extending help to laborers, handicapped individuals, and those in need can also serve as effective remedies. It's essential to recognize that Saturn calls for discipline, hard work, and patience to harness its positive influences and mitigate its challenging effects. Saturn being in the eleventh house in 2025, indicates you have duties pending for your siblings and society. You should do your duties in that regard.

Venus, as both the ruler of the Lagna (first house) and the sixth house, holds a significant position in the chart of Taurus individuals. As the ruling planet of Taurus, Venus's strength and placement play a crucial role in shaping various aspects of the native's life. An auspicious Venus bestows a range of positive attributes upon the individual. This includes good health, artistic and creative talents, physical beauty, intelligence, diplomatic skills, affectionate demeanour, gentleness, gracefulness, and reliability. The influence of Venus contributes to the native's overall charm and harmonious interactions with others. If Venus is afflicted, weak or inauspicious, then the native is devoid of good attributes as we discussed.

If Venus is not posted in the sixth, eighth or twelfth house, then the native should wear a Diamond in ring or necklace to give it strength. Those having a low sexual urge or lesser sperm and not becoming parents may consume Heera Bhasam, an Ayurvedic medicine to increase sexual urge or increase sperm count. This is generally available in all Ayurvedic stores. Advise from any Ayurvedic Doctor can be taken in this regard. Taurus native should wear good dress, use perfume, jewellery and good quality stuff in their life. Worship of Maa Durga or keeping fast on Fridays will give good results.

For Taurus natives, if there are problems at professional level, native should do remedy for Saturn.

If the Taurus natives have problem in social relationship and social recognition, they may wear yellow sapphire. However, when they wear Yellow Sapphire, it should be for certain duration and with a purpose.

In case native is having major issues in health and married life due to affliction of Jupiter, I would recommend that a cotton thread dipped in yellow turmeric be wrapped around a Peepal tree in a temple on Thursday. Planting a peepal tree in cremation ground on Thursday is found to be very effective remedy for Jupiter.

Due to afflicted Venus, the native will be addicted to gambling, alcohol, drugs, and other harmful substances. He may be a spendthrift, which could lead to poverty. The native may suffer from lack of physical appeal and amiable behaviour. An afflicted Venus creates problems in married life with a likelihood of failed marriage. This may be due to affairs with multiple partners, extra-marital relationships and divorce. A negative Venus may also cause skin diseases or diseases in body parts such as eyes, nose, chin, throat, sexual organs, kidney, bladder, etc. The natives may suffer from diabetes, addiction related to drugs, smoking and alcohol.

Some general remedies for Venus to bring about positive changes in your life. Wear clothes which are bright white. Attire in all shades of pink is also favourable. Respect your partner or spouse. Offer sweets to little girls or widowed women. Maintain good character. Attain blessings of Venus by worshipping Goddess Lakshmi. Recite the Sri Sookhtam hymn to remove obstacles and attain blessings to rise in life. Keeping fast on Friday is also beneficial. Donating on Fridays will get good results from Venus. You may donate kheer (rice pudding), curd, silver, rice and perfume.

Another significant remedy for planets in Vedic astrology is the chanting of mantras. Improve the good effects of Venus by reciting Venus Beej (Seed) Mantra - "Aum Draam Dreem Droum Sah Shukraya Namah" 108 times daily. Wear Shukra yantras to achieve auspicious results for Venus. Wear silver ornaments and perfumes, gemstones such as diamonds, opal, white topaz, etc.

Please remember that remedies are meant to address manageable planetary challenges. If a planet has more than three afflictions, it's considered as incurable or Pakka Karmas where remedies might not be effective. In such cases, individuals have to face the consequences. It is important that we have faith in God and ourselves and keep doing our deeds. By continuing to perform your actions with dedication, everything will eventually fall into its rightful place.

Wishing you another wonderful year in 2025.

PREVIOUS PREDICTIONS WHICH BECOME TRUE

In my Annual Horoscope 2024, I have made some predictions which have proved true. Regarding Earthquake during Saturn Mars conjunction from 15 Mar to 23 Apr 2024 May 2025 - An earthquake of magnitude 7.4 occurred on 02 Apr 2024 16 km S of Hualien City event in Taiwan.

I find it is difficult to find the location of earthquake. Allegation over political parties and future of AAP and Kejriwal – Lot of politicians have been maligned and Arvind Kejriwal, President of AAP was arrested and put in jail for approx. 40 days. Fire incidents and accidents in May – June 2024, large number of such incidents have happened.

Regarding BJP victory in General Elections 2024- Despite BJP slogan 400 Paar, my prediction regarding BJP has to work hard for form Government and take support of others to prove majority. BJP could get only 241 seats against the requirement of 272 so it will be forced to take support of some parties to form government. Ukraine Russia issues remain unresolved.

Ghaza, Palestine and rising support for Palestine, world is witnessing an increased support in regard to that. Conversions are on rise and the world is looking for this rise in a serious manner.

AFTERWORD

Astrology is an enchanting subject that holds the secrets of our life's purpose. If we can understand even a part of it, we are considered fortunate. Each planet influences different aspects of human life, and some effects may go beyond our logical understanding. Learning more often makes us realize how much there is to explore, like taking a spoonful of water from an ocean of knowledge.

In this book, we have attempted to provide general predictions for this zodiac sign for the year 2025. We suggest taking these predictions as warnings to prepare yourself accordingly. We may not cover everything, as there is no limit to this field. Predicting events is a complex process because of the intricate connections between planets, signs, houses, Nakshatras, and their Padas. We rely on God's blessings and use our experience and knowledge to make predictions. However, the results may vary for each person depending on their natal chart, life phase, age, background, and location.

In the predictions for 2024, I have found a large number of events happened as predicted at different places. It reinforced our belief in the science of astrology. I encourage readers to share feedback on the insights discussed in this book so that we can all learn from each other's experiences. Together, we can discover more about the fascinating world of astrology and its impact on our lives.

Please remember wheel of time is always moving. Transit of planet in one Sign or another will continue. In an earthquake, weak houses get damaged. Houses having strong foundations and structures continue to stand tall even after a strong earthquake. Similarly, those who have strong motivation, character and relationships will stand past any transit with minor vibrations. Do not worry much about the transit but make yourself strong with hard work, dedication and good deeds.

God Bless You.

****

TRANSIT OF PLANETS IN 2025

S. No	Planet	Event	Sign	Entry Date	Exit Date
1	Saturn	enters	Aquarius	18-06-2023	29-03-2025
2	Rahu	enters	Pisces	30-10-2023	18-05-2025
3	Ketu	enters	Virgo	30-10-2023	18-05-2025
4	Jupiter	Retrograde in	Taurus	09-10-2024	04-02-2025
5	Mars	enters	Cancer	20-10-2024	21-01-2025
6	Mercury	enters	Scorpio	29-10-2024	04-01-2025
7	Saturn	Direct in	Aquarius	15-11-2024	13-07-2025
8	Mars	Retrograde in	Cancer	07-12-2024	
9	Venus	enters	Aquarius	28-12-2024	28-01-2025
10	Mercury	enters	Sagittarius	04-01-2025	24-01-2025
11	Sun	enters	Capricorn	14-01-2025	12-02-2025
12	Mars	enters	Gemini	21-01-2025	03-04-2025
13	Mercury	enters	Capricorn	24-01-2025	11-02-2025
14	Venus	enters	Pisces	28-01-2025	31-05-2025
15	Jupiter	Direct in	Taurus	04-02-2025	11-11-2025
16	Mercury	enters	Aquarius	11-02-2025	27-02-2025
17	Sun	enters	Aquarius	12-02-2025	14-03-2025
18	Mars	Direct in	Gemini	24-02-2025	
19	Mercury	enters	Pisces	27-02-2025	07-05-2025
20	Venus	Retrograde in	Pisces	02-03-2025	
21	Sun	enters	Pisces	14-03-2025	14-04-2025
22	Mercury	Retrograde in	Pisces	15-03-2025	
23	Saturn	enters	Pisces	29-03-2025	03-06-2027
24	Mars	enters	Cancer	03-04-2025	07-06-2025

25	Mercury	Direct in	Pisces	07-04-2025	
26	Venus	Direct in	Pisces	13-04-2025	
27	Sun	enters	Aries	14-04-2025	15-05-2025
28	Mercury	enters	Aries	07-05-2025	23-05-2025
29	Jupiter	enters	Gemini	14-05-2025	18-10-2025
30	Sun	enters	Taurus	15-05-2025	15-06-2025
31	Rahu	enters	Aquarius	18-05-2025	05-12-2026
32	Mercury	enters	Taurus	23-05-2025	06-06-2025
33	Venus	enters	Aries	31-05-2025	29-06-2025
34	Mercury	enters	Gemini	06-06-2025	22-06-2025
35	Mars	enters	Leo	07-06-2025	28-07-2025
36	Sun	enters	Gemini	15-06-2025	16-07-2025
37	Mercury	enters	Cancer	22-06-2025	30-08-2025
38	Venus	enters	Taurus	29-06-2025	26-07-2025
39	Saturn	Retrograde in	Pisces	13-07-2025	28-11-2025
40	Sun	enters	Cancer	16-07-2025	17-08-2025
41	Mercury	Retrograde in	Cancer	18-07-2025	
42	Venus	enters	Gemini	26-07-2025	21-08-2025
43	Mars	enters	Virgo	28-07-2025	13-09-2025
44	Mercury	Direct in	Cancer	11-08-2025	
45	Sun	enters	Leo	17-08-2025	17-09-2025
46	Venus	enters	Cancer	21-08-2025	15-09-2025
47	Mercury	enters	Leo	30-08-2025	15-09-2025
48	Mars	enters	Libra	13-09-2025	27-10-2025
49	Venus	enters	Leo	15-09-2025	09-10-2025
50	Mercury	enters	Virgo	15-09-2025	03-10-2025
51	Sun	enters	Virgo	17-09-2025	17-10-2025
52	Mercury	enters	Libra	03-10-2025	24-10-2025
53	Venus	enters	Virgo	09-10-2025	02-11-2025
54	Sun	enters	Libra	17-10-2025	16-11-2025
55	Jupiter	enters	Cancer	18-10-2025	05-12-2025

56	Mercury	enters	Scorpio	24-10-2025	23-11-2025
57	Mars	enters	Scorpio	27-10-2025	07-12-2025
58	Venus	enters	Libra	02-11-2025	26-11-2025
59	Mercury	Retrograde in	Scorpio	10-11-2025	
60	Jupiter	Retrograde in	Cancer	11-11-2025	11-03-2026
61	Sun	enters	Scorpio	16-11-2025	16-12-2025
62	Mercury	enters	Libra	23-11-2025	06-12-2025
63	Venus	enters	Scorpio	26-11-2025	20-12-2025
64	Saturn	Direct in	Pisces	28-11-2025	27-07-2026
65	Mercury	Direct in	Libra	29-11-2025	
66	Jupiter	enters	Gemini	05-12-2025	02-06-2026
67	Mercury	enters	Scorpio	06-12-2025	29-12-2025
68	Mars	enters	Sagittarius	07-12-2025	16-01-2026
69	Sun	enters	Sagittarius	16-12-2025	14-01-2026
70	Venus	enters	Sagittarius	20-12-2025	13-01-2026
71	Mercury	enters	Sagittarius	29-12-2025	17-01-2026

Retrograde Details

Planet	Event	Sign	Date Entry	Date Exit
Jupiter	Direct in	Taurus	04/02/2025	11/11/2025
Jupiter	Retrograde in	Cancer	11/11/2025	11/03/2026
Mars	Direct in	Gemini	24/02/2025	
Mercury	Retrograde in	Pisces	15/03/2025	07/04/2025
Mercury	Direct in	Pisces	07/04/2025	18/07/2025
Mercury	Retrograde in	Cancer	18/07/2025	11/08/2025
Mercury	Direct in	Cancer	11/08/2025	10/11/2025
Mercury	Retrograde in	Scorpio	10/11/2025	29/11/2025
Mercury	Direct in	Libra	29/11/2025	
Saturn	Retrograde in	Pisces	13/07/2025	28/11/2025
Saturn	Direct in	Pisces	28/11/2025	27/07/2026
Venus	Retrograde in	Pisces	02/03/2025	13/04/2025
Venus	Direct in	Pisces	13/04/2025	

Eclipses in 2024-2025

S.No	Date	Eclipse Type	Area where it will be observed
1	13–14 Mar 2025	Lunar	Europe, Much of Asia, Much of Australia, Much of Africa, North America, South America, Pacific, Atlantic, Arctic, Antarctica
2	29 Mar 2025,	Solar	Europe, North in Asia, North/West Africa, Much of North America, North in South America, Atlantic, Arctic
3	07 -08 Sep 2025	Lunar	Europe, Asia, Australia, Africa, West in North America, East in South America, Pacific, Atlantic, Indian Ocean, Arctic,

			Antarctica
4	21 Sep 2025	Solar	South in Australia, Pacific, Atlantic, Antarctica

Gautam Institute of Vedic Astrology

Gautam Institute of Vedic Astrology (GIVA) has been established to enhance awareness of Vedic Astrology to those who have some interest in the subject. The purpose is to disseminate the knowledge and share it with the purpose of research and advancement of the subject. It is open to all who want to share their knowledge and those who want to learn through online classes, discussions, videos, and interactions.

Astrogiva.com, @gautamdkastrologer at YouTube, email: astrogautamdk@gmail.com

About the Authors

Dr Gautam DK, an engineer with, an MBA, MSc and Doctorate Degree in management, is from a family of Hindu Brahmins who have been engaged in astrology for centuries. Dr Gautam attended various courses as Jyotish Ratnakar, Jyotish Parveen, Jyotish Bhaskar, Jyotish Vibhushan, Jyotish Rishi, Nadi astrology, Palmistry, Vastu and Reiki Master. Now he is teaching Vedic astrology through his YouTube channel "Gautam DK Astrology" and website astrogiva.com and is involved in research on the subject. Email: astrogautamdk@gmail.com

----

Sh Naresh Gautam is the co-founder and the Chairman of GIVA. After his corporate career, he devoted himself to the field of astrology. He has been awarded the degree of Jyotish Ratan, Jyotish Bhushan, and Jyotish Prabhakar. He has been practicing astrology since the year 2000 and has a wide follower base all over the world. Due to his worldly experience, he provides very practical remedies for all the problems of life, which are not bound by fixed Karmas. Email: nareshgautam2005@gmail.com

9 798327 684355